George Martin Kober

The Fiftieth Anniversary of the Graduation in Medicine of

Samuel Clagett Busey, M.D. LL.D

George Martin Kober

The Fiftieth Anniversary of the Graduation in Medicine of Samuel Clagett Busey, M.D. LL.D

ISBN/EAN: 9783337776220

Printed in Europe, USA, Canada, Australia, Japan

Cover: Foto ©Andreas Hilbeck / pixelio.de

More available books at **www.hansebooks.com**

THE

FIFTIETH ANNIVERSARY

OF THE

GRADUATION IN MEDICINE

OF

SAMUEL CLAGETT BUSEY, M.D., LL.D.

COMPILED AND EDITED BY

GEORGE M. KOBER, M.D.

WASHINGTON, D. C., 1899

Introduction

"GOLDEN WEDDING DAY" in the practice of medicine is an event so rare and full of significance that it deserves commemoration, and in this spirit the fiftieth anniversary of Dr. Samuel C. Busey's entrance into the profession was celebrated.

The full meaning of a half-century of active professional work can only be appreciated by those who have travelled over the rough and rugged path of duty; who have watched with anxious care over the sick and witnessed the soul-stirring scenes of the death-chamber; who have faced the fury of a midnight storm to bring relief to their patients; who have gone to the haunts of poverty, speaking words of comfort and alleviating human suffering; who have braved the dangers of the battle-field and the more terrible but invisible foes of infectious diseases.

What a life of incessant physical and mental toil! What a life of self-denial and devotion!

In this glorious service, which claims the heart, mind, and hand alike, and where, alas, ingratitude is often the only recompense for duties well performed, the physician, in the midst of bitter disappointments, has but two beacon lights to guide him—his conscience and the example of the Great Physician.

Hence, what a gratification to receive upon the evening of life evidence of good-will and approval from professional brethren—a reward far more cheering and enduring than the plaudits of the multitude.

Dr. Busey, "a type of America's self-made men," has always been the friend of the struggling practitioner, and the following pages are respectfully dedicated to his colleagues, by his friend and pupil, as an encouragement in the hours of trial and despair, that they, too, may hope to profit by the ancient proverb—

Non est vivere, sed valere vita.

GEORGE M. KOBER, M.D.

Congratulatory Resolutions

AT a meeting of the Medical Society of the District of Columbia, held March 30, 1898, Dr. Thomas C. Smith, addressing the Vice-President, Dr. Kober, said in part:

"Many of us are aware that our President, Dr. Busey, will soon complete fifty years of active professional life, and it will be a fitting compliment for this body to acknowledge the event in a formal manner. I, therefore, move that a committee of three be appointed to draft suitable resolutions expressive of the esteem, etc., in which he is held."

Carried.

The Vice-President appointed Drs. Thomas C. Smith, J. Ford Thompson, and Joseph Taber Johnson as the committee.

The resolutions were submitted to the Society and unanimously adopted, at its meeting held April 6th, and were transmitted to Dr. Busey on April 8, 1898, the day of his fiftieth anniversary in medicine.

MEDICAL SOCIETY OF THE DISTRICT OF COLUMBIA,
Washington, D. C., April 8, 1898.

Dr. SAMUEL C. BUSEY,
Washington, D. C.

DEAR DOCTOR: I have the honor and pleasure of transmitting to you the following resolutions, adopted by the Medical Society on the 6th inst.:

WHEREAS, Samuel C. Busey, M.D., LL.D., President of this Society, will in a few days have passed through fifty years in the practice of medicine in this community, during which time he has faithfully served the Society as President, Censor, member of important committees, and in many other ways, and is now the only practitioner among us who has been in practice so long a period. He has always been prompt in maintaining the honor, dignity, rights, and interests of the medical profession before Congress and the community. His services in securing needed legislation for the protection of the public from ignorant and unlicensed practitioners; for the protection of physicians before the courts of law;

for the prevention of the spread of contagious diseases; and in advocating other measures which he has furthered by his industry and influence, will ever be remembered. His straightforward and honorable bearing have won for him the respect and esteem of his brethren in the profession, and his example has inspired others to emulate his fidelity. Therefore be it

Resolved, That this Society takes pleasure in calling the attention of its members to such a notable example of a career passed in the honorable and conscientious performance of its duties of life.

Resolved, That the Society trusts that many years of health and happiness may be in reserve for our esteemed President, to whom our best wishes are cordially extended.

Very respectfully,

Thomas C. Smith, M.D.,
Corresponding Secretary.

DR. THOMAS C. SMITH,

Corresponding Secretary of the Medical Society
of the District of Columbia,

MY DEAR DOCTOR : In response to your communication transmitting to me the Preamble and Resolutions of the Medical Society of the District of Columbia in commemoration of the fiftieth anniversary of my graduation in medicine, I beg that you will convey to the Society the assurance of my appreciation of the distinguished honor conferred upon me, and of the pleasure and gratification it gives me to know that my conduct and bearing through so many years have received the approval and commendation of my professional friends and colleagues.

With great respect I am

Yours, very truly,

SAMUEL C. BUSEY, M.D.

Anniversary Reception

N the evening of April 8, 1898, Dr. Busey welcomed many friends at his residence, corner of Sixteenth and I Streets, the occasion being the fiftieth anniversary of his graduation in medicine. The congratulations which were extended to the host came from many of those who have been associated with him in his career in this city during some portion at least of the past fifty years. It is given to but few men to continue for so many years in a position of such marked prominence as has been the case with him, not alone in his profession, but as a public-spirited citizen, devoted to all that pertains to the best interests of the National Capital, whose history has been enriched by his graceful pen, and its healthfulness and material prosperity promoted by his untiring efforts to secure a better water supply and more efficient methods of sanitation. Those who joined with him in the observance of this notable anniversary were, therefore, not only professional brethren, but representative men of the city.

The large and spacious home was fragrant and beautiful with floral offerings, sent by friends of a lifetime, as a greeting of affection and esteem, while there were notes and telegrams from distant friends, including one or more from the Doctor's own classmates of the University of Pennsylvania.

Among the out-of-town guests were Dr. A. Jacobi, of New York; Dr. Blackader, of Montreal, and Drs. Osler and Hurd, of the Johns Hopkins Hospital, who had come to pay special homage to the veteran physician. Every branch of professional life was represented, one of the most notable guests being Senator Morrill, of Vermont, whose eighty-eighth birthday occurred a few days later.[1]

Among the laymen present the following may be mentioned:

James G. Berret	A. R. Spofford
Alexander Graham Bell	· Charles F. Clagett
John B. Wight	William H. Clagett
Rev. Dr. T. S. Hamlin	R. Douglas Simms
Frederick L. Moore	George F. Appleby
Rev. Dr. Byron Sunderland	Worthington Bowie
Rev. Dr. Pitzer	W. F. Mattingly
W. A. Gordon	John W. Ross
Senator A. P. Gorman	Beriah Wilkins
W. B. Bryan	George W. McLanahan
Judge M. F. Morris	General John M. Wilson
Gen. John Moore, U. S. A.	B. H. Warner

[1] The *Washington Post* and *Evening Star* of April 9, 1898.

Major Robert Craig
Charles Moore
Anthony Pollok
Jeremiah M. Wilson
Calderon Carlisle
D. R. McKee
J. K. McCammon
F. P. B. Sands
Senator J. H. Gallinger
Senator Justin S. Morrill

James Morrill
Monroe Hopkins
Charles Early
James H. Saville
F. W. True
Thomas M. Chatard
Frank Hacket
W. J. McGee
Mortimer Addoms, of
New York

The physicians present were:

G. L. Magruder
W. W. Johnston
Charles W. Richardson
F. B. Loring
George N. Acker
George W. Johnston
M. F. Cuthbert
G. Wythe Cook
Z. T. Sowers
P. M. Rixey, U. S. N.
R. A. Marmion, U. S. N.
L. W. Glazebrook
H. H. Barker
W. Sinclair Bowen
Robert Fletcher, U. S. A.
H. L. E. Johnson

A. F. A. King
Thomas E. McArdle
James Dudley Morgan
Francis S. Nash
Robert Reyburn
A. Rhett Stewart
John D. Thomas
Frank Hyatt
Jos. Taber Johnson
T. Morris Murray
Ralph D. Walsh
S. S. Adams
J. H. Bryan
E. K. Goldsborough
Leigh H. French
W. M. Sprigg

James Kerr
T. Richey Stone
W. W. Godding
Francis B. Bishop
C. W. Franzoni
W. B. French
C. H. A. Kleinschmidt
G. M. Kober
Lewellyn Eliot

John S. McLain
George C. Ober
A. R. Shands
Thomas C. Smith
J. Ford Thompson
James T. Young
William C. Woodward
A. A. Snyder

Surgeon-General George M. Sternberg, U. S. A.
Assistant Surgeon-General C. H. Alden, U. S. A.
Assistant Surgeon-General W. H. Forwood, U. S. A.

In addition to the personal greetings, the Doctor received letters from all parts of the country, congratulating him upon the fiftieth anniversary of his doctorate in medicine. The following may be named from whom such letters were received:

Dr. William H. Welch .	Baltimore, Md.
Dr. Howard A. Kelly	Baltimore, Md.
Dr. William Pepper	Philadelphia, Pa.
Dr. J. F. A. Adams	Pittsfield, Mass.
Dr. J. E. Atkinson	Baltimore, Md.
Dr. John S. Billings	New York City.
Dr. John Byrne . .	Brooklyn, N. Y.
Dr. James R. Chadwick	Boston, Mass.
Dr. P. S. Conner .	Cincinnati, O.
Dr. J. M. Da Costa	Philadelphia, Pa.

Dr. W. H. Draper .	New York City.
Dr. George J. Engelman	Boston, Mass.
Dr. Bache Emmet	New York City.
Dr. R. H. Fitz .	Boston, Mass.
Dr. Thomas Flandrau .	Rome, N. Y.
Dr. C. H. Mastin .	Mobile, Ala.
Dr. I. Minis Hays	Philadelphia, Pa.
Dr. Henry Hun	Albany, N. Y.
Dr. E. W. Jenks	Detroit, Mich.
Dr. A. W. Johnston	Cincinnati, O.
Dr. Daniel A. Langhorne	Lynchburg, Va.
Dr. R. B. Maury .	Memphis, Tenn.
Dr. S. Weir Mitchell	Philadelphia, Pa.
Dr. Paul F. Mundé	New York City.
Dr. T. A. Reamy .	Cincinnati, O.
Dr. J. C. Reeve	Dayton, O.
Dr. T. M. Rotch .	Boston, Mass.
Dr. F. C. Shattuck	Boston, Mass.
Dr. A. J. C. Skene	Brooklyn, N. Y.
Dr. L. McLane Tiffany	Baltimore, Md.
Dr. H. C. Wood .	Philadelphia, Pa.
Dr. Charles H. Stowell	Lowell, Mass.
Sir William MacCormack	London, Eng.

1848   1898

Complimentary Dinner

TO

SAMUEL CLAGETT BUSEY, M.D., LL.D.

ON THE

Fiftieth Anniversary of his Graduation

BY MEMBERS OF THE

MEDICAL SOCIETY OF THE DISTRICT OF COLUMBIA

AT RAUSCHER'S, SATURDAY, APRIL 16, 1898.

COMMITTEE OF ARRANGEMENTS

Dr. JOSEPH TABER JOHNSON
Dr. J. FORD THOMPSON
Dr. W. W. JOHNSTON
Dr. THOMAS C. SMITH
Dr. C. W. FRANZONI

DEAR DOCTOR:

A number of members of the Medical Society deem it a pleasure to tender to you the compliment of a dinner at Rauscher's, on Saturday evening next at eight o'clock.

Will you kindly signify to the Committee whether the place and time indicated above will be agreeable to you?

This action is taken in view of the fact that you have just celebrated the fiftieth anniversary of your graduation in medicine, and is a spontaneous offering from your friends in the Society, who wish in this manner to manifest their appreciation of your services to the Society and the profession generally.

Awaiting your reply, I have the honor to be

Yours, very truly,

THOMAS C. SMITH, M.D.,
Secretary of the Committee.

DR. SAMUEL C. BUSEY,
901 Sixteenth Street, N. W.

901 *Sixteenth Street, N. W.,*
April 13, 1898.

Dr. Thomas C. Smith,

Dear Sir: Your polite communication tendering to me a complimentary dinner at Rauscher's, at eight o'clock, Saturday, April 16th, has been received.

It will give me great pleasure to meet the friends who tender to me the distinguished honor, at the time and place named.

Accept the assurance of my highest regard and appreciation of the compliment of the Committee and other friends.

Yours, very truly,

Samuel C. Busey, M.D.

Present at the Complimentary Dinner

N Saturday evening, April 16th, at eight o'clock, the gentlemen present assembled around the festive boards, which were arranged in the form of a horseshoe, a token of good luck to the guest of the evening.

Dr. A. F. A. King	Dr. George C. Ober
Dr. J. Ford Thompson	Dr. L. L. Friedrich
Dr. C. W. Franzoni	Dr. J. S. McLain
Dr. C. H. A. Kleinschmidt	Dr. A. R. Shands
Dr. Mary Parsons	Dr. John F. Moran
Dr. Z. T. Sowers	Dr. A. A. Hoehling, U. S. N.
Dr. W. W. Johnston	Dr. T. E. McArdle
Dr. Frank Baker	Dr. G. Lloyd Magruder
Dr. Robert Reyburn	Dr. P. M. Rixey, U. S. N.
Dr. Franck Hyatt	Dr. Robert Fletcher, U. S. A.
Dr. I. S. Stone	Dr. J. H. Bryan
Dr. H. L. E. Johnson	Dr. J. T. Young
Dr. Samuel S. Adams	Dr. L. W. Glazebrook
Dr. Thomas C. Smith	Dr. G. Wythe Cook

Dr. W. M. Sprigg   Dr. H. H. Barker
Dr. J. D. Thomas   Dr. J. Dudley Morgan
Dr. D. P. Hickling   Dr. F. S. Nash
Dr. A. E. de Schweinitz   Dr. W. C. Woodward
Dr. T. V. Hammond   Dr. J. W. Bovée
Dr. E. O. Belt   Dr. J. T. Winter
Dr. W. S. Bowen   Dr. G. N. Acker
Dr. James Kerr   Dr. Charles W. Richardson
Dr. Leigh H. French   Dr. George M. Kober

Joseph Taber Johnson

Surgeon-General George M. Sternberg, U. S. A.

Assistant Surgeon-General C. H. Alden, U. S. A.

Assistant Surgeon-General W. H. Forwood, U. S. A.

Supervising Surgeon-General W. Wyman, U. S. Marine
Hospital Service

Menu

OYSTERS–BLUE POINTS
MUSCOVITES *Sauterne*

—

CONSOMME DELIGNAC

—

MOUSSE D'YORK
OLIVES   SALTED ALMONDS   RADISHES

—

FILLETS OF STRIPED BASS, JOINVILLE
POMMES PARISIENNES   CUCUMBERS

—

SPRING LAMB, MINT SAUCE
NEW PEAS   *St. Julien*

—

SPRING CHICKEN, A LA CHEVALIERE
—   *Champagne, Louis Roderer*

SORBET LALLA ROOKH

—

SNIPES
SALAD DE SAISON

—

ASPERGES NORWEGIENNE

—

TURBANS AUX FRAISES

—

FANCY CAKES   BONBONS   PEPPERMINTS
SALTED ALMONDS   MARRON GLACES, ETC.

—

COFFEE

—

CIGARS

Toasts and Responses

D<small>R</small>. A. F. A. K<small>ING</small>, Toastmaster.

> *" Look ! he's winding up the watch of his wit ;*
> *By and by it will strike."*

1. D<small>R</small>. B<small>USEY</small>, President of the Medical Society.

D<small>R</small>. T. C. S<small>MITH</small>.

> *" Whilst the trump did sound, or drum struck up,*
> *His sword did ne'er leave striking in the field."*

2. D<small>R</small>. B<small>USEY</small>, Citizen and Sanitarian.

Surgeon-General G<small>EORGE</small> M. S<small>TERNBERG</small>.

> *" Non sibi, sed patriæ."*
> *" Till taught by pain,*
> *Men really know not what good water's worth."*

3. D<small>R</small>. B<small>USEY</small>, Physician, Author and Teacher.

D<small>R</small>. G<small>EORGE</small> M. K<small>OBER</small>.

> *" He was a scholar, and a ripe and good one ;*
> *Exceeding wise, fair-spoken and persuading."*

4. R<small>ESPONSE</small> by D<small>R</small>. B<small>USEY</small>.

ADDRESS BY DR. A. F. A. KING, TOASTMASTER.

OUR HONORED GUEST AND FRIENDS: The occasion which brings us together to-night is an extremely pleasant one; and I feel sure it is no less so to the distinguished guest in whose honor we have assembled than to ourselves.

I beg to extend to you my grateful appreciation of your kindness and good-will in selecting me to preside over your deliberations on this festive occasion, and, as you will see by the printed menu, I am indebted to the Committee of Arrangements for a suggestion of brevity in my remarks, in their intimation that I should "wind-up" before I have begun.

It gives me great pleasure to add to the general voice of the Medical Society my own congratulations to Dr. Busey on this fiftieth anniversary of his graduation in medicine.

As years roll by we all like to indulge in retrospective reviews of by-gone days, and this leads me to recall the occasion on which I first saw Dr. Busey; this was some thirty years ago.[1] I was the Recording Secretary of the Medical Society. We held our meetings in the lecture-room of the Medical Department of Georgetown University. During the proceedings on this particular occa-

---

[1] The incident referred to by Dr. King occurred soon after the reorganization of the Society, in 1866, which established the weekly meetings for the consideration of scientific subjects. Dr. Busey had not taken an active interest previous to the occasion noted by the Recording Secretary.—G. M. K.

sion a gentleman entered the hall who was unknown to me. Very soon he arose and addressed the Chair, and I was so impressed with the grace of gesture and imperious oratory with which his remarks were embellished, and which might well "command a listening Senate," that after he had concluded his speech and resumed his seat I jocosely remarked to the gentleman sitting next to me, "What *was* that?" and he told me it was Dr. S. C. Busey, whereupon I recorded his name among those in attendance at the meeting. Since that time we have all, on numerous occasions, listened with rapt attention and pleasure to our distinguished friend's impressive and finished oratory—one of the noblest gifts of God to man.

But I must not anticipate the gentlemen who are to respond to the regular toasts by enlarging upon the numerous talents and abilities of our honored guest.

What a glorious thing is age, especially when it comes to us ladened with the recollections of an honored and useful career !

When the noonday of life is passed, when its battles have been fought with courage and victory, we all like to see the evening with a sunset of gold and color and splendor. Such a conception, I think, fitly typifies the past career and present surroundings of our distinguished colleague, in whose honor we have assembled to-night.

Once more extending my congratulations and best wishes to Dr. Busey, with the hope that he may be with us for many years yet to come, I now proceed to the first of the regular toasts : "*Dr. Busey, President of the Medical Society,*" and call upon our genial Corresponding Secretary, Dr. T. C. Smith, to respond.

"Dr. Busey, President of the Medical Society."

By DR. THOMAS C. SMITH.

GENTLEMEN : I am before you to fulfil a pleasant duty, and will endeavor to express the sentiments which animate the members of the Medical Society by this testimony of our appreciation of the worth of the President of the Medical Society.

Seventy-nine years have passed since the Medical Society was incorporated, and in that time thirty-three men have served as President. What the Society has done in all these years has, to some extent, been made a matter of history by the address of Dr. W. W. Johnston, delivered at the seventy-fifth anniversary of the Society, in 1894.

In the list of names of Presidents I recall those who, in days gone by, were powers in this community. I love to think of those great men, for so I regard them. Hall, Borrows, Lieberman, Miller, Wm. P. Johnston, Toner, Tyler, Morgan, Johnson Eliot, Hagner, Palmer, Lee, Garnett, the lamented Ashford were among the number ; and I would ask if any society can produce a galaxy which will surpass these men in the attributes which go to make up character, ability, and usefulness? Do we not remember what active, useful, faithful public servants these men were until their work was arrested by sickness or other disabilities. What an amount of work was accomplished by Joseph M. Toner! What a restless, ever busy mortal was Johnson Eliot! What a mine of experience and reminiscence did we possess in Joseph Borrows! And of the others, can we not name them with enthusiasm, because of their sterling worth and of their labors to maintain the dignity and welfare of the medical profession? Truly, the Society was in good hands when these men were at the helm.

But we are here to-night to do honor to the living. We have not waited until Dr. Busey should have passed away so that resolutions of respect might be adopted. We salute him as the living, active, worthy President of the Society, and propose to tell him to his face what we think of him, for by so doing we may cheer him in his advancing years, and have him realize from day to day how his worth and work are appreciated.

What has he done as President of the Society? He has never shirked the work that has been assigned to him, and, in fact, which he has taken upon himself, when it would have more fairly devolved upon younger and physically stronger men. When it was proposed, in 1893, that the seventy-fifth anniversary of the Medical Society should be properly celebrated, who was it that was made Chairman of the Committee of Arrangements, and whose intelligence and industry made that meeting a great success? Samuel C. Busey. When it was deemed essential that the President of the Medical Society of the year 1894, whose duty it would be to preside at the anniversary, should be one who possessed the dignity, intelligence, patience, capacity, and ability to do credit to the Society, and who had the confidence of all, who was unanimously chosen to fill that office? Samuel C. Busey. And the Society has shown its good sense and appreciation of faithful service by keeping him in office ever since. When important business pertaining to the interest of the profession had to be prepared for presentation to Congress; when it was necessary to stand between the tyranny of the courts of law and the physician, jealous of his honor in maintaining inviolate the confidences of his patients; when the necessity of protecting the public against the spread of contagious diseases; when the "freaks" who infest the community raised the cry against vivisection and appealed to Congress to stop the work of the great humanitarians who are striving, by experiments on the lower animals, to devise means for protecting humanity from the fearful ravages of disease, and it was necessary to antagonize them and their work; when these and other measures needed a champion, to whom did all turn, and not vainly, for advice, support, and earnest work? Samuel C. Busey. A few years ago when a fearful accident placed the life of our friend in jeopardy, and we did not know whether we should ever see him at the Society again, deep was the sorrow of all; but a kind Providence spared him, and our joy was full when we saw him coming into the meeting, walking on crutches. Pale, emaciated, feeble, he was at his post of duty when many others were resting at home, because they did not feel like coming out. There are a great many men in the profession who after reaching the age of fifty years, more or less, conclude that there is nothing for them to do but lead lives of "innocuous desuetude," so to speak, and they settle down and wait for death to come along and knock them on the head. Not so with our President. Good and bad weather finds him at the Society, encouraging, by his presence and words, those who are trying to make the meetings interesting and profitable. He is no drone, and does not encourage such. As President of the Society, he has looked after the interests of the young men, and encouraged them to take an active part in the work of the Society, by appointing them as essayists and on committees. He is and has been the friend of the young practitioner.

Time will not permit me to say more. I have not indulged in fulsome flattery. I have spoken the truth, and you are all aware that it is only facts that I have given you.

Life is worth living if it is lived well. I believe the life our worthy President has thus far lived has been worth living, because it has been actively spent in doing those things which were for the benefit of the profession and the community.

Lacking physical vigor, as he now does, but with an active mind reaching out to find ways and means for furthering the interest of his fellow-beings, we can do no less than admire the indomitable will which dominates his frame. We extend to him our warmest greetings, and I trust that when it shall be his turn to approach the "Gates of the City," he may hear from another tongue than ours the plaudits with which we greet him to-night, "Good and faithful servant, well done."

"Dr. Busey, Citizen and Sanitarian."

By SURGEON-GENERAL GEORGE M. STERNBERG,
U. S. ARMY.

It gives me great pleasure to respond to the toast,
" Dr. Busey as a Public-spirited Citizen," because I
believe that the well-informed physician who interests
himself in the general welfare of the community in which
he lives may contribute more to the preservation of the
health of his fellow-citizens than by his ministrations
upon the sick.

The speaker then reviewed Dr. Busey's valuable
contributions to the literature of preventive medicine,
referring to his address on " The Gathering, Packing,
Transportation and Sale of Fresh Vegetables and Fruits,"
delivered at the annual meeting of the American Public
Health Association, in Philadelphia, in 1874, and to his
excellent essay on " Washington Malaria," published in
the *National Health Bulletin*, in 1882, wherein he de-
scribes not only the unsanitary local conditions which
favor the development of malaria, but also indicated how
these factors can be abated by reclaiming the river flats,
providing subsoil drainage, and hastening the completion of the sewer systems and the grading and improve-
ment of streets, together with stringent regulations
against uncemented cellars and basements. In this
essay Dr. Busey advocated the extension of the Capitol

Park south to the river shore, and its connection with the reclaimed flats along the Potomac, and many other sanitary reforms, as shown by one of his characteristic and terse sentences: "Straighten the channel of Rock Creek by cutting across the horseshoe bend at P Street; hide its filthy shores by an arch and open a park along its course; empty the Chesapeake and Ohio Canal into the Potomac above the limits of Georgetown, and destroy the unsightly observation of this cesspool of filthy water and unsavory stenches."

The speaker next referred to Dr. Busey's essay on "The Mortality of Young Children, its Causes and Prevention, and the Sanitary Care and Treatment of Children," published in 1881; "The Influence of the Constant Use of High-heeled French Shoes upon the Health and Form of the Female and upon the Relation of the Pelvic Organs," published in 1882; "The Natural Hygiene of Child-bearing Life;" his essay upon "The Wrongs of Craniotomy upon the Living Fœtus," published in 1889, and his contributions to "Morbific and Infectious Milk," published in 1895.

The speaker then reviewed Dr. Busey's achievements as President of the Medical Society and as Chairman of the Committee on Public Health, his work in urging on Congress the legislation necessary for placing the city of Washington in a satisfactory sanitary condition, and enumerated what had actually been accomplished in the way of sanitary legislation. He emphasized the fact that Dr. Busey's addresses before the Medical Society, the Board of Trade and other meetings had awakened the public and legislators to the necessity of an improved water supply and the prompt completion of the sewerage system.

The speaker referred to Dr. Busey's deep interest in the medical profession, as shown by his efforts to secure a law regulating the practice of medicine in the District of Columbia, and the law relating to the testimony of physicians in the courts; his zeal in opposing the anti-vivisection movement, and his leadership in the correction of hospital and dispensary abuses. He also referred to Dr. Busey's connection with the hospitals and other public institutions in the city, as one of the founders of the Children's and of the Garfield Hospitals, and one of the staunchest advocates for the establishment of a hospital for contagious diseases.

I have not attempted to give a complete review of Dr. Busey's life-long labors as a public-spirited citizen, but enough has been said to show that his fellow-citizens owe him a debt of gratitude for the intelligent and zealous activity which he has displayed in all matters relating to the sanitary and material interests of the city of Washington.

[Unfortunately the manuscript of General Sternberg's address was lost, and it is impossible to reproduce his remarks in full.]

Samuel le Busey
1848

"Dr. Busey, Physician, Author and Teacher."

By DR. GEORGE M. KOBER.

MR. CHAIRMAN, OUR HONORED GUEST, FRIENDS AND COLLEAGUES: There is something so remarkable in the career of the man whom we honor to-night that it may not be without a lesson to inquire into the causes of his success as a physician, author and teacher.

Whoever takes up Dr. Busey's *Souvenir* and looks at his portrait, the original of which was taken just fifty years ago, cannot fail to be impressed that the features are those of a refined, studious young man, full of seriousness, erudition and good sense—qualities which had been carefully nursed by a Christian mother and ripened under the guidance of the great teacher and physician, George Bacon Wood.

Dr. Mastin, of Mobile, Alabama, in a recent publication, in speaking of his classmate, says: " Busey was an especial favorite of Dr. Wood, and even in his youth gave promise of the distinction at which he has arrived." . . . "Although reserved and dignified, he was liked and respected by all who knew him."

The concluding sentence of this character-sketch of Busey at the age of twenty is true of him to-day.

Gifted by nature with qualities which he carefully cultivated, Dr. Busey, from the day of his graduation, was imbued with the greatness and responsibility of his calling, and fully realized that, apart from scientific attainments, the successful physician must possess purity of character, a high standard of moral excellence, and, above all, "a conscience to adjudge the penalties of ignorance and neglect."

We know by his biography that the moderate income which he inherited was scarcely sufficient to defray the necessary expenses of his education, and yet, at the age of twenty-one, he assumed the responsibilities of matrimony and established a modest home. Realizing, however, his obligation to shield his helpmate from future want, and evidently believing that every man can hammer out his own fortune, he set out in life determined to accomplish this purpose.

His brilliant professional career and the distinction which he has achieved are at once the badge and reward of all the higher and nobler attributes of the true physician.

In the practice of his profession he "united tenderness with firmness, condescension with authority," bore in silence his cares, with dignity his responsibilities, and with humility his disappointments. These qualities, together with a steadfast devotion to humanity, secured for him the confidence, gratitude and respect of his patients.

When, fifty years ago, Dr. Busey stood on the threshold of his professional life, he realized, too, that to be worthy of the high calling he had chosen, study must fill his every moment; to be successful in life, he must unceasingly study; and to gain admittance into the Temple of Fame—study, honesty and truth must be his watchwords.

How well he performed this task is shown by a list of over 163 distinct contributions to medical literature, besides his miscellaneous publications, such as his addresses, his *Reminiscences* and *Souvenir*. The world is indebted to him for his work on *Congenital Occlusion and Dilatation of Lymph Channels*, and his masterly exposition of *The Wrongs of Craniotomy upon the Living Fœtus*—writings which have long since become classic. Of his other contributions, many of which are encyclopædic, I will only say that he never wrote unless he had something to say, and he said it well.

His *Pen Pictures of the City of Washington in the Past*, indited at the age of seventy, and while in feeble health, is a monument to his literary industry, patriotism and love for truth.

It was my good fortune to meet our honored guest just twenty-five years ago as Professor of Diseases of Children in a Post Graduate course then inaugurated. One of the blessings which resulted from his connection with this school and the Department of Diseases of Children, at the Columbia Hospital, was the establishment of the Children's Hospital in this city in 1870. In fact, it may be truly said that he was the founder of Pediatric Medicine in this city. Although this school was characterized by some as an over-ambitious attempt in medical education, history shows that the promoters, of which he was one, simply planned many years ahead of their contemporaries. Nor can I refrain here from declaring that whatever success many of us have attained is due to the precepts and example of Dr. Busey as a teacher and a man; while his steadfast purpose to keep abreast with the progress of medical science, even now, is an example worthy of our emulation.

Our honored guest, notwithstanding his natural reserve and austerity, has always been the friend and leader of the struggling young practitioner. Early in the seventies he devoted his energies to the election of young men as delegates to the American Medical Association. I was present at a meeting of the Medical Association in May, 1874, when he spoke on his motion to revise the Code of Ethics and Regulations so as to conform to the Code of the American Medical Association. He ably supported the effort of Dr. J. Ford Thompson to secure consultations for female physicians and physicians of African descent, maintaining that "consultations were for the benefit of and belonged to the patient."

For similar reasons he advocated the removal of the restriction placed upon professional intercourse with army and navy surgeons stationed in this city. He vigorously protested against the admission of medical men employed as clerks in the departments, "not because they were necessarily incompetent, as had been charged by some, but from the nature of their employment they could not be thoroughly identified with the profession." At the same meeting he objected to the establishment of a maximum fee, and insisted that every physician should have the right to regulate his charges by the amount, character, and importance of the service and the ability of the patient to pay for the same.

All these and other measures of reform he prosecuted with his characteristic vigor and tenacity, and although his opponents, smarting at times under his incisive sarcasm, were pleased to speak of him as

"Busey, the dominant," no one questioned the justice of his cause, and in 1875 he was elected President of the Association.

We have simply to recall his leadership in the recent movement toward the correction of abuses in medical charities to appreciate that Dr. Busey, whether in the Chair, in the committee-room, or on the floor, has uniformly contended for the rights, honor and dignity of the medical profession.

There is no doubt that a large share of his professional success is due to a careful study and strict observance of the Code of Ethics of the American Medical Association. He was present when it was first proclaimed in the city of Philadelphia, in 1847, and his youthful mind must have been deeply impressed with the lofty tenets in which the duties of physicians to their patients, to the profession and the public are prescribed.

That he has discharged his duties to his patients is shown by the universal esteem in which he is held in the community. That he has discharged his obligations to the profession is evidenced by his sixth re-election as President of the Medical Society, and that he has filled every position of honor and trust which the profession of this city and the Association of American Physicians could confer upon him. That he has discharged his duties to the public is evinced in his contributions to preventive medicine, and the fact that during the past eight years he, with his able lieutenants in the Committee on Legislation, has been instrumental in framing and enacting seven laws in the interest of public health.

Indeed, the history of sanitation in this city is inseparably connected with that of the Medical Society and Dr. Busey as its President.

Yielding now, however, to the resistless influence of time and space, permit me, my loved and honored friend, in the name of the medical profession, to renew our hearty congratulations upon your golden wedding-day of professional life, united with the fondest hope that health and peace shall be yours till life shall end.

Hygeia will attend when years run trembling down
With honor's wreath your whitened hairs to crown,

and Minerva Medica will usher you through the portals beyond, and proudly but reverently present you to the Supreme Healer of the universe as a type of the true physician.

RESPONSE BY DR. BUSEY.

Mr. President, Friends and Colleagues: I have addressed you as friends and colleagues that I might give expression to the high regard in which I hold those who have honored me. An occasion like this is so unusual that one cannot fail to appreciate the distinction which can only come to the few who may survive the fiftieth anniversary of their graduation in medicine. When to this are added the many expressions of the good-will of my colleagues, I need not tell you how grateful I am. If I should attempt to measure my gratitude in words I fear a loosened tongue would run riot in the futile effort.

I am admonished that I must not trespass too heavily upon my strength, but there are some things that I must say even at the risk of unpleasant results.

When I came to the Presidency of the Medical Society in 1894 I made two resolutions: First, to make every effort in my power to promote the scientific progress of the Society ; and, secondly, to encourage the profession to assert itself in all matters pertaining to sanitation and preventive medicine. How far these purposes have been accomplished history must determine. I cannot, however, claim all the merit which has been so generously bestowed upon me for what has been done. To Dr. Smith much is due. He has collected and arranged the material and prepared the programmes for the weekly meetings, which I have executed, so that to him must be given the larger share of the praise for the scientific progress of the Society during the past four years. I must also share with the Committee on Legislation the success which has crowned our efforts in State medicine, in securing for this community so much in the line of preventive medicine. No one of that committee has faltered in the good work or shirked his duty, but I cannot omit mention of Drs. W. W. Johnston and Z. T. Sowers, whose very valuable services have contributed so much to promote the sanitation of the city. The Medical Society has, during the past five years, accomplished more good in this line than had been done during the previous one hundred years, and it is hoped, with the same unity and force of purpose, the progress of State medicine and public hygiene in this Capital City will be coeval with the development of scientific sanitation.

To the many kind expressions of good-will and commendation I cannot respond. They come to one who is not free from disappointment, regret and sorrow; to one not free from mistakes, who has neglected and thrown away opportunities. The chief regret of my life is that I have accomplished so little. With a prosperous beginning and fair success, I was so absorbed in the routine duties of a busy practitioner that I failed to realize the importance and magnitude of the duties of good citizenship which are incumbent upon every practitioner of medicine. If I have, during later years, sought to lead, direct and unite my colleagues in efforts to discharge their public duties, I have only partially fulfilled my obligations to you and to this community. I live in the hope that some successor will take up this line of work where I may leave it, and prosecute it with vigor and energy, to the end that our beloved profession may never again neglect or fail to assert its prerogative to advise, teach and lead the people in all measures pertaining to the preservation of health and the eradication of the causes of preventable disease.

I recall with great pleasure the success of my efforts to revise the regulations of the Medical Association of this District; the abrogation of the local Code of Ethics, which in some respects was oppressive and antagonistic to the Code of Ethics of the American Medical Association; the restoration of the *entente cordiale* between the local practitioners and the Medical Staffs of the Army and Navy, which had become strained, and the extension of the privileges of consultation to female physicians and physicians of African descent. The extension of this privilege to the classes named was hotly contested by many conspicuous members of the profession at that period. In this controversy I followed the lead of my distinguished friend, Dr. J. Ford Thompson, to whom is due the credit of initiating the reform, which, after a protracted controversy, was accomplished.

I have referred to opportunities wasted and thrown away, in that I failed to conceive the possibilities of a long life in a scientific pursuit. I was born and passed my boyhood life on a farm in a neighborhood of quiet and frugal people, who accepted the conditions and current events of life without discontent, free from the struggles, aspirations and activities of business and intellectual occupations. School-life, study, and, later, professional duty, filled the measure of my coveted acquirements. I failed to see the roadway open to all who might strive to attain distinction and honor, and when, through the partiality of professional friends, honors and opportunities came to me, I threw them away in fretful discontent, because of the interruption to the plodding routine of an active and busy life. Not until I had passed middle life did I realize the possibility of some accomplishment in the line of scientific work that might entitle me to a place among those who have contributed something to the common fund of useful knowledge. So that whatever reputation I may have acquired and may leave behind me has come through the labors of the later period of my life, and I am here to-night, as your guest, to accept the congratulations of those of my colleagues who have assembled to commemorate the fiftieth anniversary of my professional life.

In conclusion, I again thank you for this graceful compliment, and assure you of my gratitude for the many kind words spoken to me to-night.

Responses to the Invitation of the Toastmaster.

REMARKS BY Z. T. SOWERS.

MR. TOASTMASTER, OUR HONORED GUEST AND GEN-TLEMEN: You know, of course, that this call for a speech is a great surprise to me, and has caught me without any preparation whatever. I am greatly pleased, however, to be called upon, as I desire to express to you the pleasure it affords me to be with you on this interesting and memorable occasion. To celebrate the fiftieth anniversary of one's professional life rarely comes to any-one. When such an event is reached in the life of one whom we all love and honor so much as we do Dr. Busey, it becomes truly both interesting and memorable. During the past six or eight years it has been my very great pleasure to be quite intimately associated with Dr. Busey in a variety of ways, but more closely associated in the work of the Committee on Legislation, of which I have the honor to be a member. With the great labor and the happy results reached by this committee you are all familiar. The Doctor has been most kind and considerate in attributing to us much of his success; but, although we did what we could, the credit of the result should be awarded to him. He alluded to his failing strength; but while we appreciate that he may not be as strong as formerly, yet we who have been more closely associated with him are glad to know and relate that he is not so debilitated as his remarks would lead us to infer. For the comfort of those present I wish to state that I have had an opportunity of testing his condition to-night when I met him in the reception-room. He told me how feeble he was becoming; whereupon I thought I would test his strength by asking something of the Poison Bill now before Congress. If you could have heard his reply, how he analyzed it as a bill, how he related the different stages through which it had passed, and the line of argument used by him in replying to the opposition of the Pharmaceutical Association of the District of Columbia, you would, I am sure, agree with me in thinking that he is far from feeble. It has been remarked by a number of those who have spoken how much the Doctor has done to raise the Medical Society to its present exalted standing among the medical societies of this country. I fully appreciate how much he has done in this direction, and how much we are indebted to him for his great efforts, and sincerely believe that it will be greatly to the advancement of the Society if we can induce him to remain its President so long as he may live.

✳

REMARKS BY DR. JOS. TABER JOHNSON.

Mr. Toastmaster and Gentlemen: Being a member of the Committee of Arrangements I was careful to leave my name off the list of speakers in to-night's entertainment, and, therefore, think the toastmaster has exceeded his duties in calling upon me for a speech. While he has exceeded his duties in one respect he has not come up to the requirements of the occasion in others, inasmuch as he has called upon me, an unsuspecting citizen, to reply to a toast without giving him any toast or sentiment to reply to. It is fair to suppose, however, that those who have called upon me expect that the general inspiration of the occasion will furnish the theme for remarks.

Dr. Busey's abilities and reputation have been fully discussed in nearly all the directions in which he has been useful, except in the special field in which I have known him most intimately. While I have not been a member of those highly important committees which he has led to victory over the Potomac and Anacostia Flats, through the impure water supply and insufficient sewerage of the city; while I did not accompany him on his campaign against the quacks and impostors and in securing the Medical Practice Act, or in the bombardment of the anti-vivisectionists and the food adulterers, and various other campaigns for the upholding of the honor and dignity of our noble profession and the protection of the community—I say while I have not been a member of the committees under the lead of Dr. Busey for the accomplishment of these beneficent purposes—I have been associated with him more or less intimately for the past twenty-five years in the obstetrical and gynecological branches of the profession. Dr. Busey and I were together at the foundation of the American Gynecological Society twenty-three years ago, and have been side by side in many of the discussions and social functions. He was at one time Vice-President of the Society, and would have been President of it to-day had he not resigned his membership. In consideration of his distinguished abilities the Society, at its last meeting in Washington, upon my nomination, elected him an Honorary Fellow. I was present with Dr. Busey and others at the foundation of the Washington Obstetrical and Gynecological Society. He was its first President, was re-elected a fourth time, and has had much to do with shaping its policy into a successful and useful society. His known ability in parliamentary matters obtained for him from Dr. Fordyce Barker, of New York, the soubriquet of " Busey, the parliamentarian," in the American Gynecological Society. I have often wondered what Dr. Busey and others did fifty years ago, when he entered the profession, with some of the questions the successful settlement of which has added so much to the renown of obstetrics, gynecology and abdominal surgery. He practised for a number of years without those means which we have at the present day for bringing about an antiseptic environment in midwifery and gynecological surgery. It could hardly have entered his dreams fifty years ago that the mortality of childbed would have been reduced to one-sixth of one per cent., and that of ovariotomy to ten per cent. and less during his lifetime, which he has actually observed in the practice of obstetricians and gynecologists in this city. He has had the satisfaction of seeing the unnatural and abhorrent practice of craniotomy upon the living child, which he was among the first to condemn, gradually but surely give way in the onward march of abdominal surgery, until Cæsarean section has come now to be the operation of election.

Dr. Busey was among the first to recognize sepsis as the chief cause of puerperal septicæmia, or puerperal fever, as it was then called; and in a public address, when

Chairman of the Obstetric Section of the American Medical Association, called attention to the great benefits sure to follow from the more thorough practice of antiseptic midwifery. I remember hearing him read before the American Gynecological Society, in September, 1879, a most elaborate paper on the "Pathology of the Cicatrices of Pregnancy." He was also among the first to discuss on the affirmative side the unity of membranous croup and diphtheria.

I have known many instances of the most absolute confidence of Dr. Busey's patients in his advice. He has also enjoyed to a remarkable degree the confidence of his professional brethren, who have often sought his counsel. I am very glad to be here to-night and to join with the numerous friends and admirers of Dr. Busey in congratulating him upon his already long life of usefulness and many well-earned honors, and to wish for him good health and happiness for many years to come.

✱

REMARKS BY DR. W. W. JOHNSTON.

MR. TOASTMASTER AND GENTLEMEN: There is one phase of Dr. Busey's public work that has not been alluded to this evening, and it is one which is well deserving of record. I mean the part he has played in connection with the various hospitals of the District. Looking back over many years I can now see more clearly than ever that Dr. Busey's efforts were always directed to increasing the influence of the medical man in hospital management.

There have been many contests in the history of hospital work in this city, but in all of them Dr. Busey stood fairly and openly for the rights and dignity of the medical profession in hospital control.

It is necessary and unavoidable that hospital boards should be largely composed of non-medical men, but it is not right, in the discussion and decision of matters requiring expert knowledge, that physicians should have little or no part ; matters of administrative detail that deal with the medical work of the hospital can only be properly understood by physicians, and it is they who should decide all questions that concern the care of the patients, their medical and surgical treatment, the division of labor in the wards, and every matter that is of a purely technical nature. In mixed boards, where the medical staff is represented, the opportunity is given for the presentation of the medical aspect of medical questions, and the board can decide with knowledge ; but in boards composed exclusively of laymen no such opportunity is afforded, and only confusion and mismanagement result, to the great detriment of the hospital. It is natural that there should be differences of opinion, but in the free discussion of such differences, where every side can be heard, the true and best course is apt to be followed.

It is in furtherance of the best interests of hospitals that Dr. Busey has a clear record, and he deserves the thanks of the medical profession for his unswerving efforts to secure a just and fair measure of control for the physician, and for his opposition to all faulty methods of management.

But much remains to be done. It is for the men of the present and future to agitate this question until justice is secured, until the man who is most clearly interested in the beneficent work of the hospital has a just recognition of the dignity and importance of his position.

*

REMARKS BY ASSISTANT SURGEON-GENERAL
C. H. ALDEN, U. S. ARMY.

MR. CHAIRMAN: I had no idea you would call on me to-night, and I am therefore quite unprepared to speak fittingly on this occasion. One word I would like to say, however, in regard to our distinguished guest, in which I am sure I voice the sentiments of my colleagues of the medical service—a word of sincere appreciation for the part he has taken in making the members of these services in the city feel at home among you, and in bringing together the civil, military and naval members of the profession.

Dr. Busey has told us in his interesting memoirs (if I remember rightly) that military and naval surgeons were among the founders, or at least the early members, of the District Medical Society. Gradually, in the course of time, there grew up, I will not say a less cordial feeling, for the relation between the civil and military physician has always been friendly, but I may say a less intimate professional association. But I am inclined to think the fault, as well as the loss, has been chiefly on the part of the members of the two services. To Dr. Busey is largely due a change in this respect. The military and naval surgeons have been made members by invitation of the District Medical Society, encouraged to read papers and join in discussions, a privilege which I assure you has been most heartily appreciated. Social intercourse is, I think, freer than it used to be.

Dr. Busey, helpful in every measure that promises to advance his beloved profession, has taken a kindly interest in the Army Medical School, and honored us by delivering the address to the class a year ago.

I join most heartily in wishing Dr. Busey long-continued health and happiness.

*

REMARKS BY DR. A. A. HOEHLING, U. S. NAVY.

GENTLEMEN: As a representative of the Navy Medical Corps, I indorse most heartily the sentiments expressed by Dr. Alden, and I thank you for the opportunity of saying that I am proud to be an alumnus of the same medical school which graduated Professor Samuel C. Busey half a century ago ; and I wish to state that, while the venerable University of Pennsylvania reflects honor upon her graduates, Dr. Busey confers honor upon her.

*

REMARKS BY DR. SAMUEL ADAMS.

MR. TOASTMASTER : I had congratulated myself that this would be *one meeting* of the Medical Society when the Secretary could keep still ; but, as you have called on me, I cannot refrain from saying a few words in praise of our guest.

Dr. Busey was my preceptor, and I had ample opportunity for learning how to work. Soon after my graduation at the West Virginia University, in 1875, I entered Dr. Busey's office as a student. During my college life it seemed as if I had learned to study; but this belief was soon dispelled when I was brought face to face with my preceptor's untiring energies and methodical ways. Whatever capacity I now possess for hard work I attribute to the schooling received under Dr. Busey's guidance. That Dr. Busey has been an earnest worker, and that his labors have always tended toward the elevation of our profession, need no emphasis from me. I trust that his just and guiding hand will not soon cease to direct the younger men of the profession in that road which leads to success.

*

REMARKS BY DR. ROBERT REYBURN.

MR. TOASTMASTER: I am heartily glad to have been called on to say something on this occasion, for I say it from an entirely different stand-point from any of the speakers who have preceded me. Most of those who have spoken have been either pupils of Dr. Busey or at least intimately connected with him during the early years of their professional lives.

It was not so with me; in fact, our first acquaintance was made when we were direct antagonists. The Doctor and I differed very widely on political and other questions from 1872 to 1880; in fact, we do not agree on all things now. But this world would be a very stupid place if everybody agreed in everything with everybody else; and whatever antagonism we once mutually felt has long been converted into sincere and warm friendship. On this happy occasion there is but one point I wish especially to dwell upon, and that is the efforts and labors of Dr. Busey in the direction of the elevation of the medical profession of the District of Columbia.

There can be no questioning the statement that Dr. Busey has done far more toward this than any other member of the medical profession in the District. These labors will always remain as his monument, and that he may remain with us many years to see the good results of his work is my sincere desire and prayer.

✷

REMARKS BY DR. C. H. A. KLEINSCHMIDT.

MR. CHAIRMAN: The eloquent and pre-eminently truthful remarks to which we have listened with so much pleasure and the heartiest approval are the sentiments that are harbored in the breast of every member of our local society now gathered around the festive board in honor of our distinguished and beloved guest. But they are also shared by hosts of eminent professional colleagues in our country and abroad. Far be it from me to try the impossible, to add one iota to the expressions of high appreciation and devotion made to-night. But I would ask leave to recall a scene of long ago, so long that I do not care to confess to the number of years since passed. My first acquaintance by sight with Dr. Busey happened during my student days, in front of the office of my preceptor, the late Dr. John M. Snyder, who was out on the pavement ready to make his daily rounds. Somehow, during the conversation between the two gentlemen, I was strongly attracted by the stranger, and began to form certain conclusions. The brief conversation ended, and after the parting Dr. Snyder turned to me, and perhaps noting the questioning eyes, said: "That is Dr. Busey. What a great pity that a man of such prominent parts and professional ability should have retired from a successful and active career to the quiet life of a country gentleman."[1]

These remarks impressed me greatly, because spoken with earnestness and conviction ; and somehow or other the thought of Dr. Busey and his voluntary retirement and relinquishment of professional success would again and again rise in my mind.

There is, however, one point, not broached upon by any of the speakers to-night, which, to my thinking, affords the best proof, if indeed proof were wanting, of the indomitable energy always displayed in any scientific or other work, and, of course, carried to a definite and successful end. I refer to the extensive and critical investigation into the lymphatic system, from the physiological and pathological stand-point, undertaken by him a number of years ago, resulting in two monographs, embodying a collection, classification, description, and grouping of striking diseases and anomalies of the lymphatic system, a subject which at that time was receiv-

[1] Dr. Kleinschmidt's reference to the interview between Drs. Busey and Snyder may be misleading in the suggestion that Dr. Busey had retired from the practice of medicine. It is true he had changed his residence from the city to one in the suburbs north of Georgetown, on the Woodly Lane Road, known as Belvoir, but he was actively engaged in the practice of medicine in the neighborhood and contiguous country, which became so onerous that he was induced to return to the city, where the exactions of a busy professional life were less so.—G. M. K.

ing rather scant attention by the general practitioner. This extensive inquiry, of the most searching character, originated in his observation of a congenital case of a rare form of lymphatic disease, which was followed closely during life and cleared up and verified by necropsy.

Dr. Busey then conceived the idea of collecting from the medical literature of all countries cases of lymphatic diseases having a similar bearing to the one observed by himself. The task, deemed at first comparatively easy, soon became almost Herculean, in view of the class of literature found necessary to be sifted, and might have appalled many an ardent investigator. Not so with our friend. As the task grew and difficulties doubled and trebled, energy and zeal increased in direct ratio, until final success was gained in the production of the two works mentioned, embodying practically all recorded cases, but also teeming in important critical deductions and suggestions by their author.

The work of Dr. Busey is of special personal interest to me, because his kindness placed me in a position in which a better insight to his indomitable energy in scientific pursuit was afforded than would otherwise have been possible.

While in course of time the admirable characteristics of our honored guest unfolded themselves to me more and more, our acquaintance grew into friendship. There is one episode which deserves the undying gratitude of our profession. As a witness—perhaps the only one here to-night—of this striking incident, it seems eminently proper that it should be referred to on this occasion, especially as it seems to have been forgotten by many.

In the years of local confusion and strife succeeding the late war between the States our Medical Society became involved in a very serious feud with the then all-powerful Board of Health, resulting in a schism which endangered its existence, because of the determined attempts on the part of our enemies to induce Congress to repeal our charter. Defeated in this through the defence offered by Dr. Busey, as a member of our Committee, they still, nothing daunted, continued the heated controversy, and carried the contention to the American Medical Association, as the court of last resort, at its meeting in Washington in 1870. Charges, that would have been serious if well founded, were preferred against the Society, and a most determined effort made, and all means in their power were employed, to have our delegation excluded from membership in the Association.

Although prevented by service on one of the local committees from witnessing the struggle in the session of the Association, and therefore only an anxious and deeply concerned outsider, I yet did not fail to be informed by eye-witnesses of the prominent and leading part taken by Dr. Busey in that action, which again led to the defeat of the opposition ; but in the light of subsequent events this was rather a preliminary skirmish to the final battle, for the attack was renewed in Philadelphia, where it remained for the meeting in 1872 to cause the final overthrow of the factional opposition by refusing to admit to membership those who had proved enemies of our Society and attempted to destroy it by a repeal of its charter.

They came to Philadelphia apparently sure of success, and, if appearances did not deceive, it seemed to our delegates that the case would be decided by a body by no means favorably inclined toward us. Said one of my colleagues, the late Dr. Boyle, judging from what he had heard in conversation of and with members of the Association, "I am afraid they will beat us;" and in very truth, as the case was presented and discussion went on, his words seemed to be verified, for the temper of the meeting seemed to favor the opposition. But things were changed, and how completely was indifference or worse transformed! Can those who composed our small and anxious delegation at that decisive meeting ever forget the moment when our then Chairman, our guest of honor to-night, ascended the platform to address the vast audience. A hush fell on the house. Then he began quietly, calmly, and with a mien that spoke of a righteous cause. His speech was clear, incisive, and logical, and at every point presented our case with a force as convincing as truth alone can proclaim, and fairly demolished and annihilated the accusations laid against the Society, and any and all so-called facts brought forward to sustain them. How can the witnesses of that scene, which raised our spirits from despondency to hope, ever forget the storm of applause when our leader closed his speech, and the overwhelming vote by which the delegates of the opposition were refused admission, nor the feeling of relief and enthusiasm which hailed a victory verily snatched from the very jaws of defeat by the matchless argument of Dr. Busey?

In harmony with his undaunted spirit, which urged him to defend single-handed an almost forlorn cause and defeat its enemies in a fair, square, and successful struggle, is the magnanimity which he extended to them later, when, convinced of their errors, they applied for readmission to fellowship. Forgiving the past, he was the first to smoothe the way to their rehabilitation. These two striking incidents have been to me always the bright particular spots to which my mind turned when reviewing any personal reminiscences of Dr. Busey, for they illustrate most positively the brave, noble and generous qualities of his character.

Closing, I can only express the sincere wish, re-echoed, doubtless, by us all, that he may still be with us for many a year to come, an honor and ornament of our noble profession, a useful, ever alert, public-spirited citizen.

www.ingramcontent.com/pod-product-compliance
Lightning Source LLC
Chambersburg PA
CBHW031221290326
41931CB00036B/925